The Devil's Dating Game

Leon Collier

Copyright © 2022

Published in the United States of America

COPYRIGHT DISCLAIMER

All Rights Reserved. Reproduction or transmission in any form of any part of this document, mechanical or electronically, including photocopying, recording or by any information storage and retrieval system beyond that permitted in Section 107 or 108 of the 1976 United States Copyright Act is unlawful without the expressed written permission of the copyright author and publisher. International copyright laws also apply.

The Devil's Dating Game
First Edition, Paperback
Published Date: August 2022
Alpha Academic Press
ISBN: 978-1-948210-16-4

This book is dedicated to Christian singles to help them realign with God's word to ensure they get the top pick of a mate God has for them. However, they must realize that this process starts with an unwavering dedication to Christ and service as priority number one. Anything less than this renders them victims of the devil's dating game, and they will likely end up dissatisfied and have unnecessary emotional scars and baggage.

Table of Contents

COPYRIGHT DISCLAIMER 2

INTRODUCTION 5

CHAPTER 1 9

God has a plan for single Christians 9

   Serving God is at the top of the list 9

      God's plan for single Christians 10

CHAPTER 2 15

Sanctification helps single Christians see one another in a godly way 15

CHAPTER 3 19

If single Christians should not date, how will they ever find a mate? 19

      Isaac's example: 20

      God has a spouse for you. 20

      The Holy Spirit will bring your spouse into your path 20

      The Ruth Method 22

Final thoughts 26

INTRODUCTION

Why does the Bible not address dating? It is not something God intended. This book displays God's plans for Christian singles. Unfortunately, when many Christians read it, they will be shocked because they have already accepted and participated in the Devil's dating game. Therefore, they think dating is normal and harmless, but this is a delusion.

In Biblical times there was no such thing as dating; the families would play matchmakers. While this is foreign to our wicked western culture, many would be surprised to know that arranged marriages outlast many so-called marriages supposedly based on love in western culture.

Dating has been a common practice in American culture since the early 1900s.

The concept of dating began at the turn of the 20th century. Before the early 1900s, courtship was a much more private, unemotional matter. "Women would meet with several men, with her parents present, to shorten the list of potential mates down to the most suitable match for marriage, which heavily relied on factors such as financial and social status, when a young woman decided on a man she wanted to see exclusively, their activities as a couple took place either in the household or at social gatherings. At that time, there was no such thing as just two young lovers "going out on a date."

(https://www.thelist.com/62575/dating-changed-last-100-years/?utm_campaign=clip)

Since the inception of dating, a young man could visit a young lady in the African American community. Still, the family was always present, and after a particular time, the young man had to go home, which prevented potential sexual immorality. However, in the progression of time, the families unwisely allowed the "going steady" immoral trap to gain a foothold. As a result of unwanted pregnancy, many children born out of wedlock, emotionally wrecked people resulted from this wicked undertaking (dating-going steady). Some parochial schools prohibited this practice after Catholic leaders stated that "going steady" presents potential sexual immorality. A book entitled Profiles of Youth, written in the early 1950s, termed going steady a nationwide dilemma because this was the primary concern for teenagers rather than more essential concerns that should garner their attention.

Presently, single people can't be serious when meeting someone in the Devil's dating system. They must wait and watch the person for a while because they don't know what they may be getting. So, the Devil's dating system not only steers single Christians away from serving Christ, but it also puts them in vulnerable positions to be hurt emotionally, catch diseases, unwanted pregnancies, and take on the spirits carried by others.

Some readers probably ask why I call dating wicked; I ask where and when dating originated because scripture does not mention it. Therefore, it is not a biblical concept. If you want to find out the origin of dating, look at the makeup of dating. What happens in the dating game? Lust, sex, a life of immorality, and STDs. Even those who claim they are monogamous have premarital sex (fornication), which should show that dating is in line with the diabolical plan to lead young people into a life of sexual immorality with the intent to steer them away from God's plan for their lives.

An observation of the dress attire of most women in the west is a clear sign that society is morally corrupt. In the 1990s, when women wore tight body clothing, they usually wore a long shirt of some sort to cover their hips and front part. However, these days women do not cover any aspect of their bodies. They allow the world to see every curve and crevasse which only a husband should see. Unfortunately, even older women wear their tights uncovered, reflecting our society's moral decay.

Those who find my words challenging are babes in Christ. Others have blindly accepted this devilish practice (too much body exposure) due to minimal efforts to address it from a biblical perspective. A friend once said that women desire men to respect them, and men should. However, the way many women dress is confusing because they demand respect, but many of them dress like hookers. Women should dress like they want to be addressed.

In the Black community, it is embarrassing to see the way some women dress when attending church functions. Some of them dress like they are about to go to a dance club. Again, this reflects the spiritual condition of some church attendees. Therefore, it is no wonder that many of them dress provocatively like the blind sinners of the world.

Women need to realize their role in terms of temptation for their male counterparts. Men operate by sight, and when women dress so revealing, it distracts men and potentially leads their minds to sexually immoral thoughts. How can a Christian woman not be aware of this? Yet many of them have no conviction when dressing so loosely.

This ungodly way of dressing empowers the Devil's dating game to new heights and gives it an even more significant advantage over its spiritually blind victims. The Devil's dating game is the primary culprit of thousands of single-parent fatherless homes, which has left many young boys alone to navigate through life with no fatherly guidance. These boys become teenagers who assume that dating is OK. They end up impregnating young teenage girls and young women, resulting in more fatherless homes that rob young girls of much-needed father figures and protectors from the ravages of sex-driven young men.

The first generation after the 1920's who permitted the origin dating (going steady) is partly responsible for the immense problems young people are facing today, which reflects the spiritual apathy that has plagued the general church for many years. Many church attenders find this subject absurd which exposes their blindness of having accepted the world's (Devil's dating game) as an appropriate method of doing relationships. Most of them have not taken the time to seriously assess dating from a biblical perspective.

In some cases, dating leads to matrimony; however, dating often leads to heartbreak, sexual immorality, and children born out of wedlock. Bestselling author and matchmaker Hellen Chen infer that over 85% of dating ends in breakups. Satan knows that most dating will disintegrate, and heartache, regret, anger, and the fear of possibly never getting married results, which is why he loves it when singles fall into the dating game trap.

This book aims to awaken the Christian community to seriously assess dating and adopt God's plan for single Christians. The Bible instructs single Christians about God's plan for their lives to avoid immorality, emotional scars from bad relationships, and unwanted pregnancies. I will walk the readers through the scripture to demonstrate how following God's plan can give them a fulfilled life and the number one draft pick of a spouse that God has for them. For single Christians to start this process, they must be willing to rethink and reject the Devil's dating game.

Those who have fallen into the devil's dating game trap usually choose to pursue relationships and cultivate those romantic relationships above serving Christ. Their spiritual life is deplorable, which renders them powerless when serving Christ in an impactful way. Dating becomes their primary goal instead of serving Christ, which is the opposite of what the scripture recommends. The Apostle Paul writes, "…The unmarried woman cares about the things of the Lord, that she may be holy both in body and in spirit…" (1Cor. 7:34, WEB).

CHAPTER 1

God has a plan for single Christians

Serving God is at the top of the list

The unmarried woman cares about the things of the Lord that she may be holy both in body and in spirit (1Corinthians 7:34, WEB).

Christians singles #1 priority: Focused on the things of God.

Christians singles #2 priority: Living holy

Dating is not mentioned in the Bible because God has a plan for Christian singles.

Serving the Lord is supposed to be at the top of the list for Christian singles because they do not have the responsibilities of taking care of a spouse and children.

Satan loves it when single women have children outside of marriage because he knows they will not have enough time to do God's work, and therefore, they are not as much of a threat to Satan as they were before they had children.

The Apostle John says, I have written to you, fathers, because you know him who is from the beginning. I have written to you, young men, because you are strong, and the word of God remains in you, and you have overcome the evil one (1 John 2:14, WEB).

Notice the arrangement of this verse: Young men are strong; they have youth and energy. However, notice the next part of this verse, "and the word of God remains in you, which explains the last part of the verse "you have conquered the Evil One."

When you combine strength and youth with the word of God, Satan suffers defeat all the more reason why the demonic world works overtime to get young people distracted, to turn them away from Christ. And dating is one of Satan's primary tools to deter Christian singles away from doing the work of the Lord.

Therefore, the Bible does not mention dating; it encourages Christian singles to consider serving God as a top priority because they have the power to defeat the works of Satan.

God's plan for single Christians

The goal and pursuit of holiness

The unmarried woman cares about the things of the Lord that she may be holy both in body and in spirit (1Cor 7:34, WEB).

This verse indicates that their thoughts and time center around being holy both in body and spirit. In other words, single Christians are supposed to make holiness their primary concern.

However, the sinful world has spread the demonic philosophy that young people need to sow their wild oats, but this is a lie of the sinister world. Sowing one's wild oats are not more than a delay tactic the enemy uses to keep young people from living holy and serving Christ.

Germaine Copeland speaks of singles abiding in Jesus:

> One of the myths that has ensnared many single people is the mistaken idea that marriage will automatically release them from the temptation to sin. Without repentance and the renewing of the mind, those who have a problem with lustful thoughts before they are married will have the same problem after they are married, just as those who have a problem with sexual perversion before marriage will continue to have the same problem after marriage. (Germaine Copland, Prayers That Avail Much, Harrison House, Tulsa, Oklahoma, 1997, P. 159) 1

Until Christian singles get serious about their spiritual growth, their untransformed minds will continue to be ruled by lust. As a result, they will have no genuine interest in serving God and living a sexually pure life. Satan hopes that single Christians will get caught up in dating, drugs, and in things that cause them to waste their time and rob God of the service He could have gotten from them. They will deny themselves an intimate fruitful and satisfying relationship with Jesus Christ.

Don't forfeit your singleness on the Devil's beautifully colored rotten eggs. Dating is a pretty colored rotten egg that manipulates millions of single people with false promises that end in sexual immorality and negative emotional baggage.

Review of God's plan for single Christians:

1. Service

2. Sanctification

Therefore, dating is nowhere in this equation. Many church folks fall short of what God could do through them because they fail to serve Him and seriously pursue holiness. As a result, they never reach their potential as a Christian.

Young Christian singles are the greatest assets of churches, and they may be the primary reason the church is failing as a whole because they are enamored with the idea of relationships, the Devil's dating game. I did not date in high school was not because I held my present dating philosophy, but I did not because I was shy. I rededicated my life to Christ in the eleventh grade and decided at that point that if I dated, the young lady must be a Christian.

During my first year of college, I saw what I considered the girl of my dreams. She was mature, intelligent, sophisticated, and had flawless beautiful caramel brown skinned. Her smile was so soft and warm that it lit up my day. I wanted to be with her with every fiber of my being. My mind flashed into the future, and I envisioned us married and spending the rest of our lives together. I was in love with her. Because I had no dating experience, I was unsure of myself approaching her, and I became nervous every time I was around her. When we encountered each other in English class and other places on campus, I naively hoped that she would see the deep love I had for her whenever I looked into her eyes. As time progressed, the English instructor informed us about a program he wanted the class to attend in the school auditorium.

Interestingly, he told us we had to bring a guest. I immediately knew who I was going to ask to go with me. For the sake of the person's privacy, I will use an alternate name when addressing her. When class ended, I walked up to Melisa and asked her to be my guest, and she agreed. My heart leaped for joy, and I could not wait to let my roommate know that the girl of my dreams would be my guest (my first date in my mind) for the program. He rejoiced with me because he knew how much I adored Melisa and wanted to be with her. My spirit within screamed when I thought of her. I was in a daze when I looked at her and considered her qualities. I was genuinely in love with her, and though I transferred to another college at the end of the semester, I felt the love I had for her years later; I never forgot her, and others like her would always remind me of her.

I will never forget the night of the program; I nervously walked to the girl's dorm to get Melisa so we could walk to the auditorium together. I was so nervous that I tried my best to say to this sweet, beautiful mature young lady I admired dearly. My heart skipped beats numerous times on our way to the auditorium because this was my first date ever with the most beautiful woman in the world. I knew I truly loved her because I would often think of all the beautiful women in the world, and Melisa topped them all in my eyes. I also know it was true love because I did not think of her in sexual ways; I wanted her to be the love of my life for all the right reasons.

Now let me get to the point of the importance of being equally yoked. As I said earlier, I decided that I would only date a Christian at that time. On our way back from the auditorium, I asked Melisa to talk with her before going inside the dorm. She agreed, so we sat on the bench outside the dorm. I will never forget that night because it was my golden opportunity to ask Melisa if we could go steady (seriously, date). How immature for a college student, right? But remember, I had no dating experience, and because I felt so strongly for her, I was willing to give my all to her if she concurred. However, the primary requirement was that she had to be a Christian. When I asked this question, she answered yes. I breathed a sigh of relief. Now it was time to do what this present generation says, "Shoot my shot." Here's what I recall saying to Melisa:

Melisa, I have never gone on a date before, and tonight is like my first date. I don't know how to put this, but all I can tell you is that I like you a lot and I want to spend time with you. I was wondering if we could seriously date? She smiled, leaning her head to the side, and said, "Well, we can go out." She opened the door, but this was not enough for my immature mind at that time. I wanted to commit to her right there on the spot. I wanted her to see the love and admiration I had for her. She was more mature than me, and her suggestion was the right and reasonable thing to do at the time. However, I mistakenly took it as a form of rejection, and gloom quickly hovered my heart. In my mind, I thought if she only knew what was in front of her, she would have consented to my immature proposal to date seriously. Had Melisa agreed with my suggestion, I would have remained at that college until we graduated and would have married her after graduation. I am not sure how our lives would have turned out, but the love I had for her assured me that everything probably would have worked out fine.

It is clear that my adoration for Melisa was highly influential over my life, and had she agreed to be my girlfriend, she would have become like an idol in my life, no doubt, which happens to many Christian singles in the Devil's dating game. They give more attention to the person they date instead of spending sufficient time seeking holiness and serving God.

CHAPTER 2

Sanctification helps single Christians see one another in a godly way

Don't rebuke an older man but exhort him as a father; the younger men as brothers; the older women as mothers; the younger as sisters, in all purity (1Tim. 5:1-2, WEB).

God expects Christians to strive towards sanctification because this will help them look at other Christian singles as brothers and sisters in Christ rather than seeing them as potential dates. This concept is far-fetched because the church has drifted into the deep waters of sensuality and its current frame of mind makes it difficult to fathom the notion of not dating. Therefore, many Christian singles do not have the spiritual fortitude to attempt it.

Christian singles must give themselves totally to Christ and make a sincere effort to seek holiness. If they refuse to do this, the Devil's dating system lures them in and takes them down a path away from God and away from their true destiny.

The Apostle Paul infers that young people can live holy and not climb fools' hills to learn to do right. He writes, "Let no man despise your youth; but be an example to those who believe, in word, in your way of life, in love, in spirit, in faith, and purity. (1Tim. 4:12, WEB).

The word purity in this verse denotes cleanness; Paul encouraged this young pastor, Timothy, to exemplify a clean or holy life to his congregation, some of which were older than him. Paul knew that living holy as a young person amidst sinful culture was not an impossible feat.

You don't have to make a lot of mistakes to learn lessons. If you seek holiness first, you can live right without making numerous unnecessary blunders. You don't have to do many wrong things (sow your wild oats) to get all the evil out of your system during your young years and finally grow old and grow out of doing foolish things. The belief that young people have to make mistakes to learn to do right is a myth.

Paul told Timothy, a young man, to be an example. An example of this is when I accepted the call to preach as a teenager. I spent much of my time studying the Bible, my fellow church members took notice, and by the time I was a senior in high school, the pastor placed me in the older adult class, and the teacher appointed me assistant Sunday School teacher for that class. When the headteacher asked me to teach, I recall my mother sitting in my class, and this amazed me because God used me to teach my mother His word. I would ride my ten-speed bike door to door during the summer months, checking on inactive church members and praying with them. Eventually, many of those inactive members returned to the church.

I recall visiting my grandmother on one occasion, and one of her friends stopped by to see her. After the small talk, the remainder of the conversation centered around God. My grandmother's friend asked me if I would pray about her situation. She had worked for a wealthy family for many years, and they promised to give her a home. However, she thought that they might renege on their promise. I prayed for her, and two weeks later, she informed me that they had given her the house. Every time I return to my hometown, I drive by the home God gave this lady based on a teenager's prayer. The point is young Christians can make a difference for Christ if they fully commit to sanctification.

Single Christians are the greatest assets for the church and community because they do not have to make time for a spouse and children. Satan rejoices that so many single Christians get caught up in his dating game, leaving many churches lacking in many ways. Therefore, it is God's will that Christians attempt to live holy at all costs. The Apostle Paul writes, "For the purpose of God for you is this: that you may be holy, and may keep yourselves from the desires of the flesh" (1Th. 4:3, BBE). He desires that we avoid the temptation of sexual immorality; however, dating is the forbidden fruit that opens the door of erotic corruption.

CHAPTER 3

If single Christians should not date, how will they ever find a mate?

Let me start by saying you don't have to find who God has already chosen for you. The problem is that people play God when they try to find a mate. However, King Solomon says, whoever finds a wife finds a good thing and obtains favor of Yahweh (Pro. 18:22, WEB).

First, this verse says marriage is a blessing, but because so many people try to do marriage apart from how the scriptures say to do it, they end up miserable, and some end in divorce. There's no way two people stay miserable if they earnestly seek sanctification.

This verse also says that whenever a man gets married, no matter how the woman is, marriage is a good thing and puts one in a position to be blessed if the couple obeys God's word.

In this verse, King Solomon appears to say that getting married is a good thing; a wife is a good thing. Therefore, lessor emphasis is on finding a wife. Allow me to rephrase this verse: If you happen to get married or when you get married, it is a good thing, and you will be in a position to receive God's favor. Satan wants people to hate marriage to miss the blessings marriage brings.

I do not encourage single Christians to date, but I ask them to do two things that will prompt God to bring a suitable mate into their lives, and they will not waste their time dating.

Isaac's example:

Abraham made his servant promise to find a suitable (equally yoked) mate for Isaac. I will make you swear by Yahweh, the God of heaven and the God of the earth, that you shall not take a wife for my son of the daughters of the Canaanites, among whom I live. But you shall go to my country and my relatives and take a wife for my son Isaac (Ge. 24:3-4, WEB).

God has a spouse for you.

Notice that Isaac's father looked out for him to get the right kind of wife. God looks out for you to get the right kind of spouse, so you don't have to search/date. God has somebody for everybody, but many people miss their blessing because they are not living according to God's word.

The Holy Spirit will bring your spouse into your path.

When Abraham's servant (not Isaac) went to the area, the servant went, and the servant prayed and said, let the one who says and does certain things be the one God has appointed to be Isaac's wife.

In Genesis 24:44, the servant prayed, let her be the woman whom the Lord has chosen for my master's son. So, technically God chose Isaac's wife, considering the servant sought God's guidance in the process.

Therefore, Abraham, his servant, and God all played a role in acquiring a wife for Isaac. Single people, please do not miss this crucial lesson because it can determine whether you will get God's number one pick for you. However, you are bound to get one of Satan's rejects who did not get drafted if you date.

Let's look at what Isaac did in the meantime while Abraham, the servant, and God, prepared to get a wife for Isaac: Isaac went out to meditate in the field in the evening and saw camels coming (Ge. 24:63-64, WEB).

Isaac went into the field to meditate, revealing that he often spent time with God. Because he was faithful to God, He brought Isaac's wife to him; Isaac didn't have to date or look for a wife. If single Christians seriously pursue holiness, God will obligate Himself to get the mate He has already chosen for them.

My wife and I have been married more than 30 years, and I recall her having told me that before we met, she had prayed and asked God to send her a godly prospective mate, and to her delight, He brought me into her path. One of the church members I pastored introduced us, and the rest is history. We both decided that for the sake of sexual purity, I would come to see her at her father's house. By doing so, I got to know her family well, and after three months of dating, with her parent's blessings, I proposed to her on Valentine's Day with a limousine ride to an Italian restaurant. News travels fast in my wife's small hometown. One elderly lady said, "Son, what you did was so lovely; chivalry is not dead." Considering this lady's words, I think my wife got God's number one pick.

Obviously, this book does not condone dating because it is not biblical; however, the intent is to help Christian singles line up with God's word concerning this matter, serving, and trusting Him to bring His number one pick as a marriage partner for life into their lives.

The Ruth Method

The following is a word of wisdom for single Christian women. If you follow Ruth's example, God will ensure you get the number one pick for a husband. A few things need to be done to make this happen.

#1. Connect with faithful Christian women rather than partying church girls

Then they lifted up their voices and wept again; and Orpah kissed her mother-in-law, but Ruth clung to her (Ru. 1:14, RSV). Orpah decided to return to her homeland and idol gods (Ru. 1:15). To worship idols is to worship demons (Deut.32:17; 1Cor. 10:20). Therefore, Orpah may have married again, but I am sure she did not get God's number one pick because she worshipped idols. Chemosh (fish god) was the national deity of the Moabites, whose name meant "destroyer," this was the god of the Moabites, according to Judges 11:24. The Learn Religions site offers more insight regarding this god Orpah worshipped:

> Chemosh seems to have also had a taste for blood. In 2Kings 3:27 we find that human sacrifice was part of the rites of Chemosh. This practice, while gruesome, was certainly not unique to the Moabites, as such rites were commonplace in the various Canaanite religious cults, including those of the Baals and Moloch.
>
> https://www.learnreligions.com/chemosh-lord-of-the-moabites-117630

The International Standard Bible Encyclopedia referred to Chemosh as the abomination of Moab. The point I am making is that Orpah returned to worship a cursed idol, which would negatively affect her life one way or another. However, Ruth decided to stay with Naomi, who worshipped the One true God. She stated, "Give up requesting me to go away from you, or to go back without you: for where you go, I will go, and where you take your rest, I will take my rest; your people will be my people, and your God my God" (Ru. 1:16, BBE).

#2. When you connect with godly people, never leave them

Where you die, I will die, and there I will be buried. May the LORD do so to me, and more also, if anything but death parts you and me Ru. 1:17, (MKJV).

Ruth also committed to the One true God through Naomi, which would change her life tremendously. Ruth eventually married Boaz, a relative of Naomi and from this marriage descended David and our Savior Jesus Christ (Mt 1:5). Because Ruth remained connected to Naomi and decided to worship the God of Naomi, her life was never the same. By the way, the name Ruth means "satisfied." Therefore, she became content because she connected with a godly woman and committed to God, putting her in the lineage of Jesus Christ. It is also noteworthy to mention that a book in the Bible is named after her.

When Ruth made the wise choice to remain connected to Naomi and serve the one true God, she positioned herself to gain a godly husband. After solidifying her connection to Naomi, Ruth became industrious to labor for her and her mother-in-law (Ruth 2:2), much like Isaac. He focused on God and his responsibilities rather than seeking relationships (Genesis 24:63), aligning with Apostle Paul's recommendation for Christian singles. He writes, "But I desire to have you to be free from cares. He who is unmarried is concerned for the things of the Lord, how he may please the Lord" (1Cor. 7:32, WEB). Satan desires that Christian singles chase after relationships and not serve God. In doing so, they unintentionally and unknowingly forfeit the mate God has in mind for them. As Ruth focused on her responsibilities, God fixed it to where a godly man noticed her: Then Boaz said to his servant who was in authority over the cutters, whose girl is this? (Ru. 2:5, BBE). When we put God first and be responsible, He takes the initiative to bring the right people into our path.

Boaz noticed and highlighted what Ruth had done for her mother-in-law and her faith in God (Ru. 2:11-18), and the fact that she had not chased after other men (Ru. 3:10). Let this be a lesson to single women; men take notice of descent women of quality. They are the ones men want to marry rather than a half-naked loose girl that sleeps around. If Christian singles serve God faithfully, He will bring people into their lives that honor and appreciate their sacrifices.

Naomi advised Ruth how to present herself to get Boaz's attention. The New Testament charges older Christian women with teaching younger women. The Apostle writes:

> Older women likewise be reverent in behavior, not slanderers nor enslaved to much wine, teachers of that which is good; that they may train the young women to love their husbands, to love their children, to be sober minded, chaste, workers at home, kind, being in subjection to their own husbands, that God's word may not be blasphemed (Titus 2:3-5, WEB).

Some older church women are spiritual babies in the western world, much like the younger women. They wear revealing and provocative body-tight clothing in public, thus promoting lust. It is no wonder many women find it challenging to find good and godly marriage prospects. A social meeting saying declares, "Dress how you want to be addressed." Another states, "A classy lady turns heads with all her clothes on." Ruth was blessed to have a wise, godly older woman in her life to offer sound advice, which benefited Ruth. King Solomon writes, "...in an abundance of counselors there is victory (Pro. 24:6b, RSV).

The Apostle Peter weighs in on this issue; he writes:

> Let your beauty be not just the outward adorning of braiding the hair, and of wearing jewels of gold, or of putting on fine clothing; but in the hidden person of the heart, in the incorruptible adornment of a gentle and quiet spirit, which is in the sight of God very precious. For this is how the holy women before, who hoped in God also adorned themselves... (1Ptr 3:3-5a, WEB).

This text does not dismiss proper outward adorning, but it sets a precedence that Christian women should place greater emphasis on inner beauty. Jesus said, "Life is more than food..." (Lk. 12: 23, WEB). The Greek word for "life" is psuche, which means breath or soul. Therefore, greater emphasis is placed on the inner condition instead of the outer condition. Christian singles should do their best to ensure their inner condition is as attractive as their outward appearance because this means more to God and potential spouses in the long run.

Final thoughts

The need for discernment

Dear friends, do not believe every spirit, but test the spirits to see whether they are from God, because many false prophets have gone out into the world (1John 4:1, NIV).

While this verse encourages Christians to beware of those who teach false doctrine, it can also apply to knowing the spirits of people who are disingenuous.

Sanctification not only makes it possible for God to bring the number one pick (mate) into your path, but it will also grant you stronger discernment to know the spirits of those you meet. In the Devil's dating game, many folks end up disappointed because Satan disguises himself well and presents an attractive first impression to lure in the victim. The point is, if Christian singles seek holiness first and serving God, the Holy Spirit will speak to their hearts and reveal the real person behind the mask. 95% of Christian singles do not have discernment of the Holy Spirit because they do not seriously pursue holiness.

The first step in doing relationships the way the Bible describes is to confess our sins (1John 1:9) and try to abide in God's word daily (John 14:27). Germaine Copeland offers the following prayer for singles who desire to abide in Christ and have His word abide in them:

> Lord, I am abiding in your word holding fast to your teachings and living in accordance with them. It is my desire to be Your true disciple. I am abiding in the vine. I cannot bear fruit unless I abide in you...Lord, you have assured me that if I keep your commandments, I will abide in your love and live in it, just as Your Son, Jesus, obeyed Your commandments and lived in your love. He told me these things, that your joy and delight may be in me and that my joy and gladness may be of full measure and

overflowing...I have hidden your word in my heart that I might not sin against You. May Christ through my faith dwell in my heart! It is my desire to be rooted deep in love and founded securely on love, that I may have the power and be strong to apprehend and grasp with all the saints what is the breadth and length and height and depth of it. I pray, in the name of Jesus, that I may know this love that surpasses knowledge-that I may be filled to the measure of all Your fullness. Now to You, who are able to do immeasurably more than all I ask or imagine, according to Your power that is at work within me, to You be the glory in the church and in Christ Jesus throughout all generations, forever and ever! Amen. (Germaine Copland, Prayers That Avail Much, Harrison House, Tulsa, Oklahoma, 1997, Pp. 161, 162) 2

NOTES:

www.ingramcontent.com/pod-product-compliance
Lightning Source LLC
Chambersburg PA
CBHW070755050426
42449CB00010B/2491